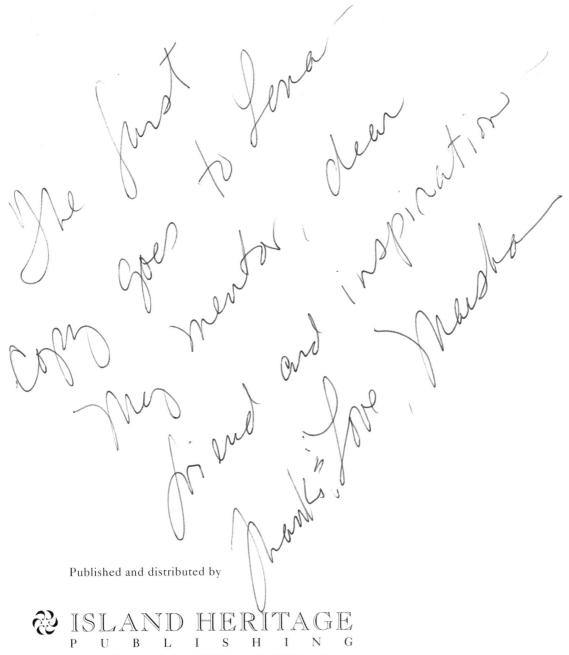

The first to Lena
copy goes to dear
My mentor
friend and inspiration
thanks, love Marsha

Published and distributed by

ISLAND HERITAGE
PUBLISHING

94-411 KŌ'AKI STREET, WAIPAHU, HAWAI'I 96797
Orders: (800) 468-2800 • Information: (808) 564-8800
Fax: (808) 564-8877
www.islandheritage.com

ISBN# : 0-89610-375-7

First Edition, First Printing - 2001

Lei Aloha

Flower Lei of Hawai'i with Instructions

Marsha Heckman

ISLAND HERITAGE

Dedication

Lei Aloha is dedicated to Floyd,
for bringing me to Hawai`i,
and Wendy, Julian, and Ken
for giving me a Kaua`i home.

contents

Acknowledgements

Mahalo to Irmalee Pomroy for her guidance and instruction, and her generosity in helping make sure *Lei Aloha* was accurate and respectful. I am most grateful for her friendship.

To the *lei* makers I have been honored to know: Lola, Ken and Sam Bukoski were first to show me how to make a *lei*. Their mother, Elizabeth, was my first Hawaiian teacher.

The *lei* makers who contributed their beautiful work to *Lei Aloha*: Alison Ah Puck, Marina Pascua, Nancy Fuertes Fuller, Kalei Cadawas, Majorie Dente, Randy Akau, Uli'i Castor, Cads Samio, David Chang and Royal Hawaiian Leis.

Mahalo to the artists responsible for the results of my vision: Micki Fletcher and Ronnda Heinrich.

Mahalo to the people who graciously shared their experience with me: Fern Delos Santos and Dora Brown Martinez of Dora's Lei Stand.

Also to Walter, Paul and Neolani Pomroy, Mamo Ornellas and Laverne Bishop.

I am grateful for the information and inspiration I gained from the work of Marie Leilehua McDonald, and other writers: Marie Neal, Lorraine Kuch, Laurie Shimizu Ide and Angela Kay Kepler, and the University of Hawai'i Oral History Project. Thank you Patty Lei Belcher and the staff of the Library of the Bishop Museum for the help and guidance.

foreword

Sitting on a garden bench outside the front door of my Hawaiian homestead farmhouse, Marsha Heckman speaks fondly of her work with flowers as a designer, of gardens, and of her new found love—the *lei*, the floral garlands of Hawai'i.

Coming to Kaua'i for the first time in 1992 after a devastating storm had ripped through our island devouring most of the beautiful flora, Marsha came back again and again viewing the slow return of Kaua'i's beauty to what it is today, lush and breathtakingly beautiful.

Two days prior to our sitting on the garden bench, Marsha Heckman, a complete stranger, introduced herself over the phone and asked me to speak with her about *na lei* Hawai'i. Her appreciation for the mountains and valleys, the seashore and ocean, and the people of Hawai'i touched me. Her feelings for the *lei*, with her descriptions and her desires, were so profound. She was discovering the *lei*. I could immediately sense she was having a love affair with the *lei*. I was living the *lei* and I could understand her profound affection for *na lei* Hawai'i, and her desire to simply, elegantly share them with everyone through her book, *Lei Aloha*.

Usually I wait awhile and think about things, but I just jumped in when Marsha asked me to advise her. The *lei* brings people together, two strangers become everlasting friends. I love her book. The stories in *Lei Aloha* tell us how deeply involved one can get when working with the *lei*. These oral histories are folk stories to be treasured. *Lei Aloha* has recognized the *lei* as a premier treasure Hawai'i offers to the world. *Lei Aloha* honors the *lei* makers, it honors Hawai'i. She sought *lei* makers and brings their crafts and their stories for all to enjoy and cherish.

Cherish the *lei* as she does. Cherish the *lei* as I do.

Irmalee Kamakaonaona A. Pomroy
Mea hana lei
Anahola, Kaua'i, Hawai'i

Irmalee Pomroy is an internationally-known lei maker and is the sister of master lei maker and author Marie McDonald. Irmalee has represented Kaua'i and the state of Hawai'i in numerous statewide, national, and international celebrations and competitions. She has lectured and demonstrated lei making at the Honolulu Academy of Arts, the Bishop Museum, the National Tropical Botanical Gardens, Kaua'i Historical Society, Kōke'e Natural History Museum, the University of Hawai'i–Mānoa Campus and Kaua'i Community College. The Kaua'i Museum May Day lei contest was started by Irmalee Pomroy 20 years ago.

introduction

I came to Kaua'i when my daughter, Wendy, married Ken Bukoski. He took me to meet his Hawaiian mother, Elizabeth, and I watched her string *'ilima* flowers picked from the bushes in her front yard. Ken gave me a *lei* like a string of hand carved ivory beads, each shaped like a tiny crown. I had never seen a flower like it.

The night before the wedding a pig was roasting in the *imu* (an oven in the ground), and Ken's family gathered around two big tables to make the *lei* for the wedding. (I was told then the plural of *lei* is properly *lei*.) The brothers had been to the mountains to pick *mokihana* and *maile*. They pulled the bunched-up clumps of leaves out of canvas saddlebags and stretched them out on the table. *Maile* had the most wonderful woodsy vanilla smell.

The men began "talking story" and tying the strands together. Lola and Elaine and Uli'i were stringing little green seedpods that also smelled delicious—like warm anise. This was the lei of the island of Kaua'i, *mokihana*. While Rosie wrapped the *lei* in ti leaves, Lola made ginger buds into lei for the mothers in the Micronesian

Lei *maker stringing plumeria blossoms.*

Keiki (*children*) hula *dancers wearing ti leaf skirt and plumeria* lei *on head, neck, and wrists.*

9

style. My *lei* looked like a scalloped macramé necklace with a ruffle that bloomed while I was wearing it.

The groom's *lei* was beautiful, thick leafy strands of *maile* wrapped with ropes of *mokihana*. It hung from his shoulders open-ended, down to his knees. Elizabeth wore her strings of 1,500 little *'ilima* blossoms. The guests brought *lei* to the wedding, wore them and gave them to friends with a warm smile and a kiss. It seemed to me the reward for making a *lei* was in the giving of it to someone. I came to find out that is the "*aloha* spirit." The *lei* embodies the *aloha* spirit of the Hawaiian people. It is their warmth as much as the warm sun that brings us back again and again. Many of us never leave. A *lei* is given in that spirit—warmth, hospitality, love, peace, hello, farewell. A *lei* can say good luck, congratulations, I love you, I honor you, thank you.

Wendy took me to a May Day *lei* competition in Līhu'e. I did not know a *lei* could be so breathtaking, I had never seen many of these flowers—beautiful *'ohai ali'i*, delicate *pakalana*, and the astonishing turquoise blossom of the jade vine. Hawai'i is a subtropical island with wonderful growing conditions. It has 2,500 flowering plants. Of these, 900 are endemic, found in the Hawaiian Islands and nowhere else. One hundred are indigenous, plants at home in the islands but which came naturally from somewhere else—on the wind, with birds, or by storm. About 1,500 were introduced to Hawai'i indirectly or directly by man.

Hawaiians will make a *lei* with any leaf or flower that will hold up awhile when picked. If it doesn't stink or stick or stain, they will string or braid it into a garland for the neck or head. They embraced each new flower and created a new *lei* with it.

I was amazed at the display of *lei* at the Kaua'i Museum on May Day. Each *lei* I saw was more gorgeous than the last. The flowers were braided with ferns and seeds, leaves were fashioned into roses and ropes. There was a *lei* of 10 long strings of fragrant *pīkake*, each bud as tiny as a pearl. The work, artistry and beauty were extraordinary. I wanted to take home a picture of every *lei* to look at forever.

I introduced myself to several of the *lei* makers and exclaimed over their entries. I appreciated their work, their design talents, their beautiful flowers. They appreciated my praise. In researching and writing *Lei Aloha*, I have come to appreciate

Hawai'i profoundly. The beauty of the land has infused its people with a gracefulness that shows in the making and giving of *lei*. I treasure the friends I have made of the *lei* makers who contributed to *Lei Aloha*, we feel the kinship of flower lovers. My work is with flowers, I write about flowers. I wanted to own a book with beautiful photographs and stories about the flowers and people who make the *lei*.

My advisor for *Lei Aloha* is *lei* maker Irmalee Pomroy. She teaches and demonstrates "...for the *aloha*." Nancy Fuller makes *lei* "....for the sharing." Dora Martinez because "...it makes people happy." Marina Pascua, "....to show the beauty of the flowers." Kalei Cadawas told me to "Express your gratitude to the place," and David Chang gives it away because, "You know somebody loves you when they give you that *lei*."

The flowers may last only a few hours, but the memory of having a *lei* placed on your shoulders lasts forever. I wrote this book in honor of Hawai'i's *lei* makers.

Marsha Heckman
June, 2001
Kaua'i

A remarkable sight is King Kamehameha's statue draped with 26 foot long lei of every kind on King Kamehameha Day.

Dancers wearing maile lei, *sacred to Laka, goddess of the* hula.

11

representing the islands

*C*ertain plants became the symbols of each island over time because they flourished on that island or had a legendary meaning particular to that place. Hawai'i's Territorial Legislature adopted *"Na Lei 'o Hawai'i"* in 1923 and officially designated a color and *lei* to represent each island. Six are plants known since ancient Hawai'i: *'Ilima* for O'ahu, Kaua'i's *mokihana*, the *kukui* for Moloka'i, red *lehua* on Hawai'i, Kaho'olawe has the *hinahina*, and Lāna'i is represented by the *kauna'oa* vine. The islanders of Maui loved the rose, *loke*. It is the only flower brought by settlers to officially represent an island. The eighth is Ni'ihau; the dry little island has its treasured Columbella shells or *pūpū* Ni'ihau, which like *mokihana*, are found nowhere else on earth.

Pā'ū Riders

For celebrations of the Merrie Monarch Festival, King Kamehameha Day and Aloha Week, there are pageants across the Islands with music, *hula*, and parades. *Pā'ū* riders provide the pageantry. Groups on horseback represent an island by wearing its color and its official *lei*. The riders and their horses are decked with the most extravagant display of *lei*: riders wear several around their neck and shoulders, and usually wrapped around their head. Massive amounts of flowers and greens decorate the horses and their tack and saddles. Coveted awards are given in a competition with stringent rules. *Pā'ū* riders are judged on horsemanship, unity and performance, and for the creativity and ingenuity of horse and rider's adornments. A jury chooses a princess from each group and assigns the riders an island to represent in the parade.

Ni'ihau—*pūpū shells (white)*
Kaua'i—*mokihana (purple)*
O'ahu—*'ilima (yellow)*
Maui—*loke (pink)*
Kaho'olawe—*hinahina (silver-gray)*
Lāna'i—*kauna'oa (orange)*
Moloka'i—*kukui (green)*
Hawai'i—*lehua (red)*

lei maker's art

Two writers get the credit for suggesting one of Hawai'i's most beloved celebrations. Poet Don Blanding proposed in an article for a Honolulu newspaper that the old island custom of making and wearing a *lei* should be celebrated. Grace Tower Warren's suggestion was "May Day is Lei Day". In 1929 the Governor proclaimed that residents "Observe the day and honor the traditions of Hawai'i." The *Honolulu Star-Bulletin* front page read: "Lei Day recaptured the old spirit of the islands....a love of color and flowers, fragrance, laughter, and aloha." Every year the celebrations include a May Day royal court with princesses representing each island, music, exhibitions of *hula*, *lei* stands, and the *lei*-making competitions. On May Day everyone wears a *lei*.

The May Day competitions are often intense, with innovative designs and traditional *lei* of the finest workmanship and the freshest flowers. *Lei* makers compete for the ribbons and prizes in categories defined by color, plus there are many special awards. The display on every island on May Day is the ultimate in the Hawaiian *lei* maker's art.

The *lei* makers who won prizes in the May Day competitions all over Hawai'i in 2001 created astonishing new designs and gorgeous interpretations within the strict guidelines. Each year they outdo the previous winners with new ways to use the Islands' bounty of flowers for the *lei aloha*.

A truck covered with hundreds of lei *is a platform for dancers in a May Day (Lei Day) parade.*

Randy Akau
loke (rose) *lei*

Randy's prize-winning lei *is roses, ferns, and* hinahina *attached to a raffia cord.*

Randy Akau's Hawaiian grandmother inspired him and showed him how to make *lei*. The rose was her favorite flower. He entered the Honolulu May Day *lei* contest the first time in 2000. "I never thought I was good enough, but I made the rose *lei* in her honor and won the theme award." The beautiful *loke lani haku lei* is Randy's specialty and he won again in 2001 with the splendid display of roses in his *lei*.

Ti is the sacred symbol of the gods and an emblem of divine power.

Marjorie Dente
Kipu'upu'u

Marjorie has been making ti leaf *lei* for more than 20 years. She won the Kaua'i Museum Trustees Prestigious Award with her ti *lei*.

"This is not a traditional *lei*. I named it after I made it because it turned out to be such a strong *lei*, and such a male *lei*. I named it *Kipu'upu'u* for the special warriors in Kamehameha's time. I really enjoy making *lei* for men because that part of me can come out in the *lei*, that strength, that strength of maleness. I'm inspired mostly by the material itself, and being able to feel whatever energy comes through. I feel very blessed to have the luxury of bringing my idea to fruition. I feel totally fulfilled."

"The *lei* is made with red, green, and yellow leaves, of course the yellow leaf is a green leaf ready to drop off the plant. The main braid is two yellow strands and two green ones in a round braid I learned in Girl Scouts. I stitched that onto a backing of eight green twists and stitched all that together in a tier style so it would lay flat. The fringe is 60 red leaves, pressed in the middle so I could fold them over, then looped through one of the green twists, and tied. I fringe each leaf first with my finger nails."

Three colors of ti leaves are twisted, braided, and fringed in this masculine lei.

17

Kalei Cadawas

Seven ribbons went to Kalei Cadawas for his May Day 2001 *lei*. He also designs and makes all the *lei* for one prize-winning team of *pā'ū* riders and horses in the May Day parade.

"There is no date when I started to make *lei*. There was never a time when I was not surrounded by flowers because of my mother. She had a hothouse and a garden. She never wore makeup, but she always had a flower in her hair. She passed on and I wanted to continue remembering her. This was a way. I didn't know I had a talent. I started fiddling with flowers and I said, 'Wow I can really do this, and it doesn't look half bad!' "

"When I make a *lei* I think about where the *lei* is gonna go. What the purpose is. Who the *lei* is for. What is this expression of myself going to do that transcends the *lei*? I think about the smiles that I'll see, the love that it's going to bring, the happiness."

ti *lei*

"It's just *wili*," Kalei says, as if this *lei* were simple. "The leaves are twisted, then braided, *hili*, to make a certain length. That's a nine-strand *lei* of darker green leaves, braided in three sets, put together to make the base. The rosettes and the main braid on top contrast, bringing out the beautiful colors of the different leaves. The top braid is floated on the base. I let it flow along the lei and attached it where I felt it would be nice to accent with a rosette. The rosettes are secured with raffia. I use only natural materials because that is more in tune with the whole *lei* experience."

Kalei attached the top braid to the base of his lei with ti leaf rosettes.

multi-colored *lei*

"Most important is the protocol of asking the place where you gather, and really feeling gratitude for what is taken, and leaving a *hoʻokupu*, a gift. I love the cultivation and gathering, selecting the materials for my *lei*. All of the *ʻohana*, the family of the *lei* maker and all of the friends, are always so willing to give their prized flowers just so they can be part of your *lei*. I feel each person, the love given to me, are part of my *lei*."

"I was thinking about something different and innovative. I wanted to be articulate. I wanted to bring something that nobody had done before. I can't begin to tell you how many flowers are in this *lei*. All different colors and textures, all chosen for beauty. I made it *wili*. Flowers are bound with raffia on a center cord. I think the *lei* describes me, a really colorful person. I thought about all the people in Hawaiʻi, all the different cultures in the melting pot we have here. That's what I think about when I make the many color *lei*."

Kalei used as many as twenty varieties of flowers and greens in this gorgeous winning entry.

Marina Pascua

May Day of 2001 is the first year Marina Pascua entered the *Lei* Day contest. Her *lei* made from the petals of the red "jungle king" ginger won the prestigious Ginger Alexander Award at the Kaua'i Museum May Day competition, and her stephanotis *"kahili lei"* won first prize in the white *lei* division.

kahili lei

"You have to show the beauty of the flowers as well as the structure. Before I make *lei* I meditate and ask God to guide my hands, give me sharp eyes to see."

Marina had an image in mind for her original stephanotis *lei* design. "I was thinking of the *kahili*—the feather emblem of the *ali'i*. I strung the petals to look feathery, like the *kahili*. I cut off 1/8" of the tube with the stem, and made three strands to connect each *kahili*. In *ikebana* you use odd numbers, and you don't waste anything that is part of the flower."

Marina strung the stephanotis to imitate the feather top of the ceremonial kahili.

23

red ginger *lei*

"Everyone makes feminine *lei* but for men it was always the leaves—the ti, *maile*, green ferns. I wanted to make a flower *lei* for a man. Movement was important. Males move around more than females. Ginger is strong, but *hinahina* will soften it a bit. Preparation was hard. You pick the head of the ginger and soak it in water. Then wash and pluck the leaves, sort by the size. Trim the petals to make it neat. I folded the petals and sewed four of them into crosses like pinwheels. I sewed them on top of each other, alternating the ones made with small petals then the larger. I put in the *hinahina*, but it looked too busy. I took a single *hinahina* strand and wrapped it around the string between the flowers. That stabilized the pinwheel. I looked at that *lei* and I said, 'You, you are strong, strong like a man.'"

The red ginger came from Malaysia and is the most common ginger in Hawaiian gardens.

Marina chose the ginger for its strong red color.

Nancy Fuertes Fuller

For 20 years Nancy has won ribbons on May Day for her *lei*-making skill and designs. "You're not entering for the prize, you're entering to share what you have learned. You want to show the people who come the different ways you can work with flowers, and help people appreciate the flowers around our island. That's the beauty of weaving a *lei*."

yellow orchid *lei*

Nancy will tell you she has a reputation. "They say 'No matter where she goes, she'll find flowers and try to put them together'. It may be a legend, but it's true." She made the yellow *lei* with ferns from Kōke'e, orchids from her friend Irene's garden, and the little yellow flowers are "By the fence of the airport parking lot," she says with a big smile. "The *lei* is *wili*, you just wrap it with raffia."

Nancy combines several varieties of flowers selected for their complementary colors in her elegant lei.

Lola Bukoski

Turn into Lola's driveway and you are flanked by plumeria trees of every color, strawberry red, lemon yellow, and one like rainbow sherbet. Through the trees on the right is a long row of 'ilima bushes, patiently watered every morning. Hibiscus and bright red and yellow 'ohai ali'i flowers tip the trees behind the plumeria, and in front of the house is a room-size patch of orchids. Lola gets her ferns from the shady wall under the overhang next to her Mickey Mouse tree with its red faces and beady black eyes.

There are few flowers Lola needs to make her lei that aren't growing in this garden, but just in case, she could pick up gardenias and pīkake and pua kenikeni from Sam's mother's place next door. On the shady side of the lanai is a lava rock wall crawling with wild pea vines with little pink flowers for the maunaloa lei. In a sunny spot behind the house baby's breath blooms underneath a tall trellis of chartreuse clusters of pakalana, heavy with honeybees.

Follow a low fence covered with budding stephanotis past a white ginger hedge heading toward the back pasture to the "Kōke'e" garden. Lola's husband Sam has planted red lehua and yellow lehua bushes and a rare mountain hibiscus. For three years he has nurtured a little maile vine that seems to be surviving under the guava tree. Out by the dog kennel Sam has a kitchen garden —taro, lemon grass, comfrey, sage, rosemary, chives, and Hawaiian chili peppers. Behind the herbs there are mango and banana trees shading a stand of ti plants for lei materials. Butterflies visit crown flowers growing on the lawn and Lola is at her table making another lei.

Lei maker Lola Bukoski grows most of the flowers she uses in her own garden.

haku lei

"I make haku the traditional way. I use raffia instead of hau to keep from making it too thick. I just braid everything I like together."

Lei of Old Hawai'i

The history of the Hawaiian *lei* begins with the Polynesians who traveled the Pacific in canoes, navigating by the stars. When they found Hawai'i they had animals and plants from their home in the southern seas with them: useful, hardy plants for food and medicine and building, but they also brought a flower, ginger, for decoration and adornment. The Polynesians were lei makers. They made wreaths to honor their gods and strung flowers and vines to drape their bodies on ceremonial occasions and whenever it moved them. Everything in nature came by the grace of the gods, so plants were dedicated to them and considered sacred. Reverence and gratitude for the land is an integral part of Hawaiian life.

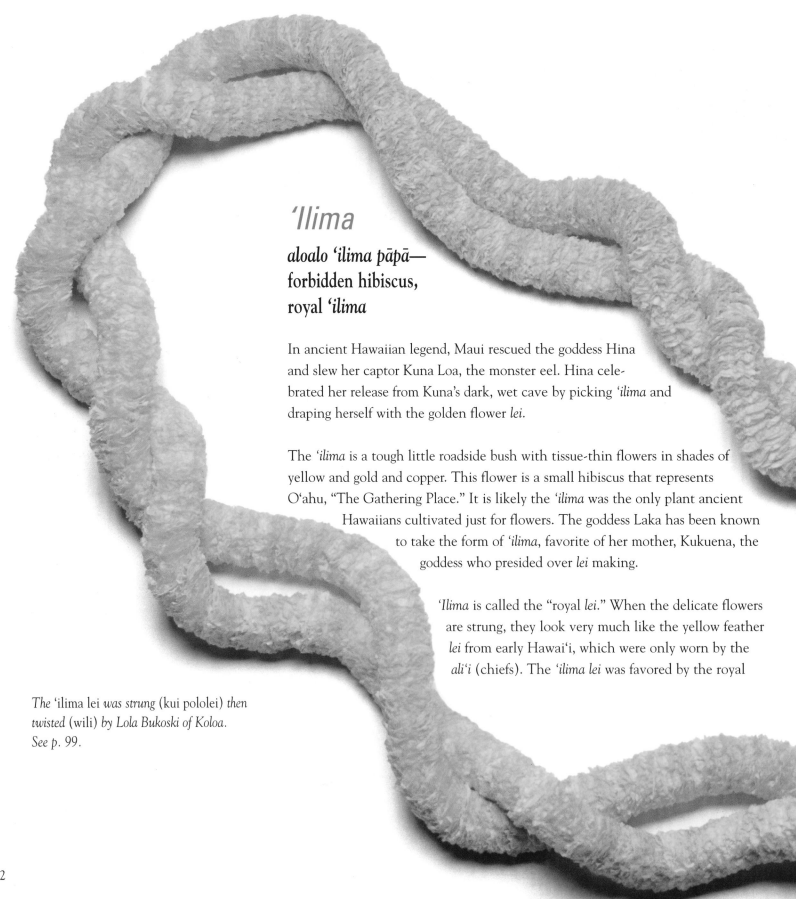

'Ilima

aloalo 'ilima pāpā—forbidden hibiscus, royal 'ilima

In ancient Hawaiian legend, Maui rescued the goddess Hina and slew her captor Kuna Loa, the monster eel. Hina celebrated her release from Kuna's dark, wet cave by picking *'ilima* and draping herself with the golden flower *lei*.

The *'ilima* is a tough little roadside bush with tissue-thin flowers in shades of yellow and gold and copper. This flower is a small hibiscus that represents O'ahu, "The Gathering Place." It is likely the *'ilima* was the only plant ancient Hawaiians cultivated just for flowers. The goddess Laka has been known to take the form of *'ilima*, favorite of her mother, Kukuena, the goddess who presided over *lei* making.

'Ilima is called the "royal *lei*." When the delicate flowers are strung, they look very much like the yellow feather *lei* from early Hawai'i, which were only worn by the *ali'i* (chiefs). The *'ilima lei* was favored by the royal

The 'ilima lei *was strung (kui pololei) then twisted (wili) by Lola Bukoski of Koloa.* *See p. 99.*

'Ilima *is called the "royal lei" and was traditionally presented to those of high rank, but anybody may wear an 'ilima lei.*

Most lei makers prefer to gather the 'ilima flowers before the sun comes up. It is painstaking labor to pick and string 700 blossoms for a single neck lei which lasts only one day.

family and was the *lei* most often presented to those of high rank. A *lei* might be yards long, each *ali'i* wearing several. How many ladies in waiting must have worked all night to gather and string the thousands of blossoms to make such a *lei*?

A common person was never to put hands above the head of a royal person, so to present a *lei* to the *ali'i* involved protocol. The *lei* would be untied, and one side held, perhaps by an attendant, while the other hand brought the *lei* around the royal shoulders. The *'ilima lei* is associated with royalty, but anybody can wear one.

The useful kukui originated in Asia and traveled to the Spice Islands of Indonesia, and the Marquesas and Society Islands. Kukui represents Moloka'i, "The Friendly Isle," and is the State Tree of Hawai'i.

The kukui leaves and flowers are braided (hili) by Uli'i Castor of Kōloa.

Kukui
candlenut tree

In the dark green mountain forests throughout Hawai'i, the pale green *kukui* shimmers on the landscape. Its fluttering silver-green leaves cluster in the gullies and hug hillsides on every island. A revered *kukui* growing near the house provides shade, fuel, food and medicine, beautiful leaves and flowers for a *lei*.

Precious *kukui* seeds were carried in the canoes that brought the Polynesians to the Hawaiian Islands long ago. Those ancient sailors chewed a *kukui* nut and spit on the water for a clear view. Ancient Hawaiians oiled their surfboards with *kukui* nut oil, and fishermen lit their way with *kukui* nut torches in the pre-dawn darkness. Oily *kukui* nuts were strung on a bamboo sliver and burned to provide light. Root, leaves, and sap were used to heal rashes and blisters. Their fishing nets, tanned with *kukui* bark, lasted for years, and canoes were stained with a dye made by burning the nut and mixing it with the oil.

Polynesians used a tool made of fish bone and the same dye to tattoo their bodies, a custom enthusiastically copied by European sailors. And Hawaiians say the *menehune*, a race of little people who were legendary early residents of the Islands, played a game with spinning tops made from *kukui* nuts.

Pā'ū rider wears kukui nut lei and lei of kukui leaves and flowers representing Moloka'i.

Lehua

'ōhi'a lehua, lehua 'āpane (red), lehua mamo (yellow)

Namakaokaha'i, goddess of the sea, defeated her sister, Pele, goddess of fire, and chased her across the ocean all the way from Tahiti to Hawai'i. Pele searched for a safe place to hide her sacred fire, the source of her power. Namakaokaha'i attacked her with a storm and drove her from Kaua'i. Pele fled to O'ahu only to be flooded, and escaping to Moloka'i, she was hunted down again. On the island of Maui, Pele faced fierce Namakaokaha'i. A horrific battle ended with Pele apparently dead. But the Goddess had hidden her sacred fire deep inside Kīlauea Volcano on the island of Hawai'i, far from the shore where the sea could never reach. And her spirit rose and flew to Kīlauea where she still makes her presence known.

The scarlet *lehua* is sacred to Pele, goddess of fire and the volcanoes. When Pele first arrived in Hawai'i, she placed a *lei lehua* on the little island west of Ni'ihau, giving it its name. A *lei lehua* is a proper offering for Pele, but permission is necessary before picking the blossoms. Hawaiians never pick on the way up the mountain for fear of rain and Pele's retribution. They make an offering at the mountaintop, and make a *lei* on the way down to show where they have been and their devotion to her.

Island deities make their home in sacred forests on the slopes of the steep green mountains. 'Ōhi'a is a sacred forest tree. The dense wood of its twisted trunk was used for temple carvings and offerings to the gods, but only with permission of the chief. *Lehua* is a symbol of strength and is also the flower which represents Hawai'i, the "Volcano Island."

The lehua is arranged in a braid (haku) *with raffia. The young leaves and buds* (liko lehua) *and seed capsules* (hua lehua) *are part of the* lei *made by Nancy Fuller of Po'ipū.*

'Ōhi'a is from the same family as guava. Some 'ōhi'a lehua flowers are pink, salmon, or even white. Lehua mamo is yellow, named for the extinct mamo bird, whose yellow feathers were of the highest value in old Hawai'i. Lehua 'āpane is named for the Hawaiian honey-creeper or 'apapane, a bird whose red feathers are used in featherwork.

Like certain seaweeds, kauna'oa *was worn as a lei when visiting the seashore.*

Kauna'oa
kauna'oa kahakai—beach orphan vine, orange dodder

The *kauna'oa* vine was a gift the goddess Pele left on the beaches of the Hawaiian Islands. *Kauna'oa* is a yellow-orange parasite from the morning glory family whose stems grow like a web over shrubs and fields and beaches. Its scientific name (Cuscuta Sandwichiana) means "tangled twist of hair from the Sandwich Islands." Its flowers are so small they are barely visible, and it has no leaves at all. *Kauna'oa* represents Lana'i, the "Pineapple Island."

Lei maker Nancy Fuller was asked to make a *kauna'oa lei* for a May Day princess with *kauna'oa* vines. The girl's parents brought vines from Kaua'i, where she was born. They also gave Nancy *kauna'oa* from the mother's home on Lana'i, and a piece from the "Big Island" of Hawai'i where Dad grew up. Nancy made the *lei* only to discover the strands had separated from each other during the night. "I think the *kauna'oa* wants to stay only with its island neighbor." She twisted the *lei* again only to see it unravel before it could be placed on the girl's shoulders at the pageant.

The kauna'oa lei *was twisted* (wili) *by Alison Ah Puck, of Honolulu, and the braided* (hili) *lei with ferns was made by Nancy Fuller of Po'ipū.*

The Barren Isle

For centuries this island was populated by Hawaiian people, and was a private ranch just prior to World War II. At that time, Kahoʻolawe was taken over by the United States Navy and used as a training ground and bombing range for the next 50 years. Hawaiians began referring to the uninhabited island as the "Island of Death". Ravaged by goats, wind, lack of care, shelling, troop maneuvers, and a simulated atomic bomb blast, it was left treeless, scarred red earth.

In the last decade, the island has become a symbol of a Hawaiian cultural renaissance. The tireless efforts groups like the "Protect Kahoʻolawe ʻOhana" have made to reclaim Kahoʻolawe have been successful. The State of Hawaiʻi is now the official owner of the island. The bombing was stopped in 1990 and November 11, 2003 is the deadline for the 10-year, $400 million clean-up by the U.S. Navy.

Plans to reverse the damage are being put into action. Four hundred people took part in a healing ceremony when the island was returned to Hawaiʻi. Native plants were brought back and elders from all the Hawaiian Islands participated in the rituals. Kahoʻolawe has been designated a cultural and natural reserve for the preservation and practice of all cultural and spiritual rights exercised by native Hawaiians. Only educational, scientific, and cultural activities can take place there now.

The hinahina lei was braided (hili) by Alison Ah Puck of Honolulu. See p. 102.

Hinahina

**'āhinahina, Pele's hair, Spanish Moss,
'umi'umi-o-Dole—Dole's beard**

The plant representing Kaho'olawe, "The Barren Island," is a hard-to-find beach heliotrope with tiny white and yellow flowers and silver-green leaves and stems. The air plant from the pineapple family commonly called Spanish Moss, is a substitute for the beach heliotrope, and both are called *hinahina*, the Hawaiian word for their silvery-gray color.

Kaho'olawe is considered the sacred home of Kanaloa, the god of the ocean. It is believed to be the island where Kanaloa first arrived in Hawai'i. We know from a very long ancient Hawaiian chant that Kaho'olawe had great significance because star navigation was taught on the mountain, Moa'ulaiki. It was their ability to navigate by the stars that made it possible for Polynesians to travel the vast Pacific.

On Kaho'olawe the heliotrope was obliterated by a goat population introduced to the island. Now it is growing again on Moa'ulanui, the highest peak on Kaho'olawe. Rene Silva, a native Hawaiian, is given credit for the replanting effort begun 20 years ago to reintroduce native species to the island. The Maui locals refer to him as their "Hawaiian Johnny Appleseed."

Hinahina—*beach heliotrope.*

Pele's hair is a substitute hinahina.

Pūpū Niʻihau
Niʻihau shell, Columbella, *momi*

The "Island of Yesterday," Niʻihau, and its little neighbor, Lehua Island, have been privately owned for more than a century. The people of Niʻihau have kept to many of the old Hawaiian ways because their island is not open to visitors. These few hundred residents fish, cultivate honey, produce charcoal, and raise sheep for their livelihood. And they are famous for stringing the beautiful Niʻihau shell *lei*.

During winter, the islanders gather the rare *Columbella* seashells for the *lei* which represents Niʻihau. Storms bring high surf that washes these shells onto the sandy beaches and rocky shoreline of the island. During the calmer months, Islanders sort the shells they call *momi* and make them into *lei* as perfect and beautiful as a string of pearls from Tiffany.

During Victorian times, the lustrous shell *lei* were as desired as pearls by Hawaiʻi's royalty. Queen Kapiolani and Queen Emma wore many strands of the treasured Niʻihau *lei* with their long dresses. Shell *lei* are popular throughout Polynesia, worn in Tonga, Tahiti, Samoa and Fiji, but none are as valued or admired as the *pūpū Niʻihau lei*. When a woman is betrothed on Niʻihau, she begins to string her bridal *lei* a year before the wedding. The *lei* is supposed to be 20 strands, an impressive dowry.

Pāʻū riders representing Niʻihau wear multiple strands of rare Columbella shells.

Niʻihau shell lei loaned by Nancy Fuller from her collection.

Caution must be used when stringing moki-hana—it can burn skin and eyes. Mokihana is almost always strung with strands of maile; combining the two makes a beautiful, long-lasting scent. It cannot be exported.

Mokihana
Pelea anisata

Named for Pele, goddess of the volcano, this slender tree grows exclusively in the forests on Kaua'i. *Mokihana* is loved for its spicy aroma much like anise, which stays with the seed pods for years. The *mokihana* has been used to perfume *kapa*, the Hawaiian tapa cloth, since ancient times. A string of these leathery green "berries" is the most treasured seed *lei* because of its rarity. *Mokihana* is one of about 50 native Hawaiian species of 'alani, (orange trees). Its fragrant fruit is symbolic of Kaua'i, "The Garden Isle." A *lei* of *mokihana* is seldom seen on the other islands. *Mokihana* is becoming scarce and there is concern this rare species may become endangered.

Mokihana *is strung* (kui) *entwined with a knotted* (kīpuʻu) *maile lei* made by Lola Bukoski of Koloa. *Her husband, Sam, and his brother Ken picked the vines and "berries" deep in the mountains of Kōkeʻe.*

Strands of fragrant mokihana *drape a* pāʻū *rider representing Kauaʻi.*

45

A Kaua'i Story

"My father, Pua Okina, was the one who took me up the mountain. I was his pet and his little shadow. I rode in front of him on his horse." Elizabeth closes her eyes and looks back three quarters of a century. "He showed me how to dry the salt, gather the maile and mokihana, to fish and pick up opihi, prepare the imu."

"My mother was called Elikapeka—but she didn't have a true Hawaiian name. In those days the Hawaiians were discriminated against by the white people, so she had a white name—Elizabeth. My mother was the daughter of James Sinclair, disowned by his family for marrying a full-blooded Hawaiian woman."

Elizabeth has lived on Kaua'i all her life. "My father and mother were going up to Wai'ale'ale to pick *maile* and *mokihana*, my mother riding a white horse named Maggie. When they were going she began to labor, so my father told Maggie to take Mama home and stay there at Waihulu. She never reach there, she labored to have me right up there on the mountain. My father came to her and wrapped me in the horse blanket."

"My father told my mother to give me a name, she called me Elizabeth, like her. My father gave me my Hawaiian name—Kalehuamakanoe, the name of the place where I was born, and the name of the *lehua* that blooms up there."

Young Elizabeth loved school. "In my mind I made a goal that I would be a teacher, so I was set on going to high school. But my mother was in the hospital a long time, and my father stayed on the mountain. I told my uncle, 'I like stay here and go to school'. He and my aunty had no children, so they took me and my sister and brother to live with them. I finished, ready to go to high school, but my uncle said I had to go work on the plantation."

"I picked up cane, worked in the ditch, everything. Frank Bukoski was the man who supplied the cane to the mill, he was back and forth all the time on his big horse. I fell in love with him because I couldn't go to school. We got married and had six children. I taught my children to pick *maile* and *mokihana*, and make the Kaua'i *lei*, but only Sam and Kenneth have the knack of it."

"My dad told me, and I told my kids, 'Whenever you go to the mountain, don't be greedy. If you gonna leave the seeds there, they gonna grow more. You just take enough to use'." Elizabeth is concerned that there will be *mokihana* for her great-grandchildren to pick. "Only what you need," she warns. "That's all. If you can make the *lei* on the mountain, mo' better. Take lunch, make a *lei*. After you wear the *mokihana lei* you can use it for camphor. I put with my quilts and no bugs will come. It makes the quilt smell good."

Ken and Sam Bukoski went up into the mountains of Kōke'e on horseback in search of the *mokihana* berries and *maile* for the *lei* pictured. A lifetime of hunting pig and mountain goat, as well as gathering plants on the mountain with their mother tells them where they will find it.

Dancers wearing the maile lei *tell their story in the* hula *they perform.*

maile

Elders say if you smell *maile* where none is growing, you may be near the remains of an ancient temple to the goddess of the *hula*, Laka. *Maile* is sacred to her, it is always offered at her alter and worn by those who honor Laka in the dance. She could assume the form of a *maile* vine at will, and left the magical scent behind when she departed.

Before the *hula* begins, there is a graceful dressing ceremony. Chanting the ritual *mele*, dancers move together to tie an anklet of *maile* on each leg, then in unison—the skirt, and last the *lei*, on neck and head. The preparation for the dance is a dance itself. A *maile lei* is presented to the goddess, and placed with reverence on her altar.

Called maile *in Hawai'i and Samoa,* maire *in the Cook Islands and Tahiti. Three varieties grow in the Islands: on Hawai'i the large leaf,* maile lau nui; *O'ahu has a medium leaf,* maile lau li'i; *and the most desirable, from Kaua'i, has very small leaves,* maile lau li'ili'i.

Noblest of all *lei*, and most favored by the old Hawaiians, *maile* is associated with worshipping gods. But the *lei* can be worn by anyone—especially to celebrate. *Maile* has an unforgettable woodsy vanilla smell, thought to have magical power. The fragrance lingers for weeks after the *maile* has dried.

Maile *is knotted* (kīpu'u) *then the strands twisted* (wili) *together. See p. 98.*

In the tropic moonlight, the "Old Folks"—ghosts—wander with the wind through the valleys of the island of Hawai'i. *Paniolos* (cowboys) say that when the "Old Folks" pass by on the trails at night, they can smell *maile*. The horses move aside and stand absolutely still in the dark. They sniff the air until the eerie parade has drifted down the road.

The hula dancer wears flower lei *and* maile, *which is sacred to Laka, goddess of hula.*

Ti leaf was used for wrapping, cooking and storing food, and to make thatch, rope, sandals, raincoats, fly whisks and whistles. A lei is carried in a bag made of ti leaves.

Ti
kī, lā'ī

Ti is the sacred symbol of the gods and an emblem of divine power. The *kahuna* (priests) still wear a *lei* of two ti leaves tied together at the back of the neck. In keeping with its spiritual symbolism, the ti plant has power over evil. Hawaiians planted ti around their homes and temples to keep bad spirits away and hold good fortune inside.

On ceremonial occasions a stalk of ti was carried to announce the presence of royalty. Over time it evolved into the *kahili*, a polished wood pole topped with intricate feather work in the likeness of a ti plant. This royal standard accompanied the *ali'i* and provided protection.

Ti leaf lei is twisted (wili). *See p. 96.*

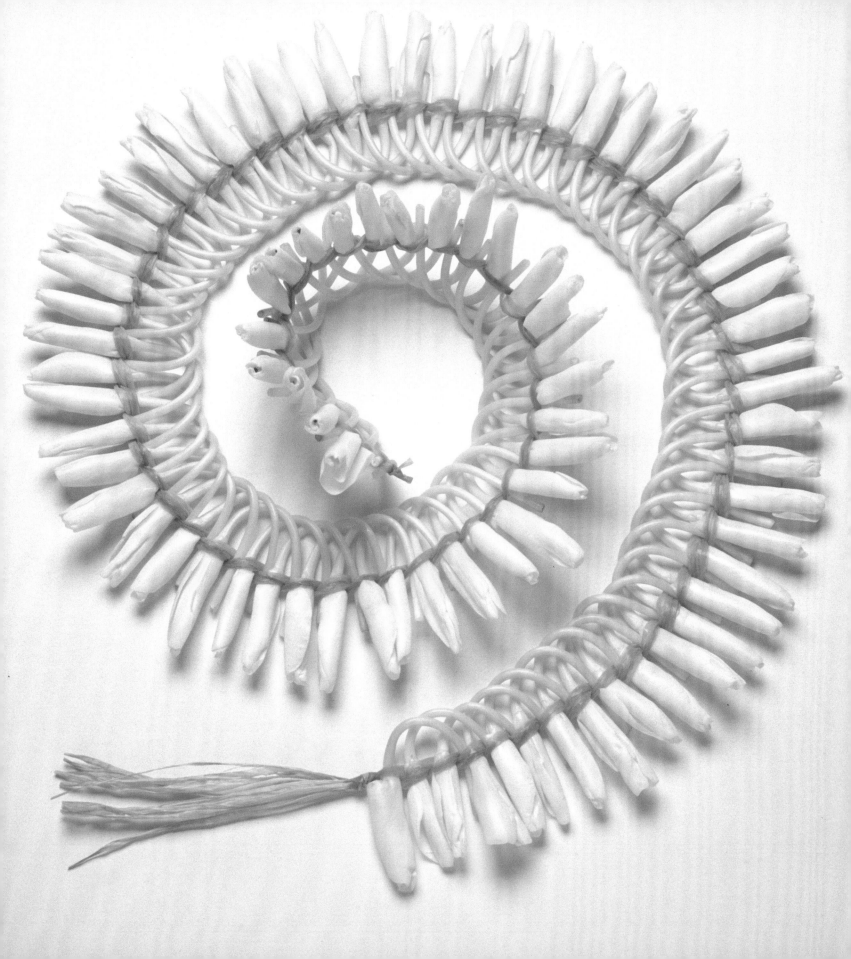

'Awapuhi-Ke'oke'o
white ginger, ginger lily, butterfly lily, garland flower

A ginger was believed to be the one plant brought to the Hawaiian Islands by the Polynesians for making *lei*. These explorers carried plants with multiple practical uses and medicinal qualities, or for food. But they included ginger for the pleasure of its perfume and decorative beauty. This exotic scented white ginger is cultivated in the Islands and grows wild in India. White ginger *lei* are as highly regarded there as in Hawai'i. The white ginger *lei* is called an "evening *lei*", its seductive perfume suggests lovemaking.

The Micronesian-style ginger *lei* was demonstrated by *lei* maker Lynn Martin. She shared her technique of plaiting an intricate design with the ginger buds in the workshops she teaches on culture and the arts. She traces the necklace-style *lei* to the people of the Western Pacific Yap Islands. A simplified version of her *lei* is a favorite of Hawaiians and visitors.

White ginger is a source of perfume produced commercially in Hawai'i.

White ginger buds are tied Micronesian-style to make this lei. *See p. 103.*

19th Century Lei

Immigration began with the
Polynesian seafarers about 500 A.D.,
but the landing of Captain Cook in
1778 began more than a century of
immigration from all over the world to
the "Sandwich Islands" of Hawai'i.
Missionaries from America came to
convert the Hawaiians and brought
roses. Chinese came to work the cane
fields and planted orchids, *pakalana*,
and *pīkake*. Bougainvillea arrived from
Mexico, plumeria from Tahiti, jade
vine from the Phillippines. Hawaiians
have only seven consonants in their
language, so the names of the new
flowers were "Hawaiianized"—
kalaunu for crown, *pukanawila* for
bougainvillea, *loke* for rose.

Loke lani
rose of heaven, *loke*, damask rose, China rose, Maui rose

The Missionaries who came to Maui, "the Valley Island", brought bare-root rose bushes from America with them. They built New England-style houses and planted roses to remind them of gardens at home. Immigrants from Asia also brought the beloved rose to the Islands, and they flourished here. Hawaiian people appreciated the long-lasting buds for the *lei*, and were enamored with their wonderful scent and beautiful form.

The rose was particularly beloved by Maui islanders, who chose the pink damask rose to represent their island. It is the only island flower designate that was brought to Hawai'i in modern times. Tragically, infestation of the rose beetle destroyed most of the older roses in Hawai'i, but replacements are thriving today.

The rose lei is strung lengthwise through the center (kui pololei) by Alison Ah Puck of Honolulu.

Na Lei 'o ka Loke

Randy Akau's family is from Hana, Maui. It was his grandmother who inspired him to make *lei*. "*Tutu* taught me to ride horse, to make *lei*. I was her tail, and her favorite." Randy's grandmother loved roses. "My grandmother's *lei* was not uniform, but it was her. She used any rose, any color, open or closed."

"Every year I was invited to enter the *lei* contest. I would enter, my *tutu* made the *lei*, I would win. When I was a senior in high school they decided to have everyone make the *lei* there—on site at the contest!" Horrified, Randy began to make his first *lei* in front of the judges and everyone. They thought he had made *lei* all his life.

"But my hands just knew how to make it because I had watched my grandmother's hands." Randy entered the Honolulu May Day *lei* competition the first time last year. "I never thought I was good enough, but that was the year my *tutu* died and the theme was '*Na Lei 'o ka Loke*'. I made the rose *lei* in her honor and won the theme award."

Randy took his rose *lei* to his grandmother's grave and placed it on her headstone. "When you make *lei* to honor someone, remembering her while you make it, the *lei* carries more special meaning and expresses your love."

Pua kenikeni
ten-cent flower, dime flower, *pua* tree

The pua tree is a member of the strychnine family.

"Ten-cent flower" was the name given by the *lei* sellers who worked the Honolulu Harbor docks. When a strand of 65 crown flowers or 50 plumeria sold for a quarter, this *lei* was very dear at 10 cents a bloom.

The *pua* tree is a South Pacific native, first planted in a garden in Oʻahu at the end of the 19th Century. Hawaiians embraced the flowers, loving to see them bloom creamy white then turn to butter yellow and golden orange by the end of the day. The smell of *pua kenikeni* is heavenly; Tahitians infuse coconut oil with the blossoms for a tropical perfume.

The corolla tube is cut to one inch and the pua kenikeni *is single-strung* (kui pololei).

ʻOhai aliʻi
royal tree, dwarf poinciana, chief's poinciana, Pride of Barbados

The beautiful crimson and vibrant yellow poinciana blooms reminded Hawaiians of the magnificent feather cloaks and helmets worn by the Monarchy. They called it *ʻohai aliʻi*— royal tree.

Lei made with great difficulty, or with rare flowers or feathers were for the highest ranking chiefs. The tiny tufts of yellow on the thigh and tail of the black *mamo*, a honeycreeper bird, and the paler yellow from the *ʻoʻo* were the most prized feathers. The red-headed *ʻiʻiwi* and *ʻapapane* supplied red feathers, the other royal color.

It took great ingenuity and skill to trap the bright forest birds. Bird catchers and feather crafters had a guild, *poʻe kahai manu*, and were esteemed professionals. They studied bird movements and habits diligently. They spied on nests to catch baby birds and take their downy feathers before they learned to fly. Inventive methods—bird poles, sticky traps, "mist nets," and bird whistles—were used to catch some birds, who were released after giving up their yellow or red feathers. Others were hunted, snared or stoned, then eaten after their feathers were taken.

Poinciana was brought to Hawaiʻi early in the nineteenth century from the Caribbean. The ʻohai aliʻi cannot be exported to the mainland.

The ʻohai aliʻi is strung crosswise, round (kui poepoe).

59

Lei *maker Davis Pa demonstrates the Micronesian style.*

Turk's cap hibiscus
aloalo pahūpahū—firecracker hibiscus, *lei* hibiscus

The Turk's cap hibiscus is a native of Mexico.

The hibiscus is Hawai'i's State Flower. More than 30 native species of hibiscus grew profusely on the Islands. The flowers are edible and make beautiful decoration for rituals and feasts. A Hawaiian would drink hibiscus tea and make an infusion with hibiscus that was medicine for many ailments and a refreshing tonic for purifying the blood. They extracted a purple dye from the flower and painted intricate designs on *kapa* (tapa cloth). When Hawai'i was a territory its emblem was a *koki'o'ula*, a native red hibiscus, but the official State hibiscus is yellow, *ma'o hau hele*, an endangered native.

Most hibiscus flowers wilt when picked so they are rarely used for making *lei*. But the bright scarlet blooms of this variety never fully open and do not wilt as easily. The Turk's cap hibiscus *lei* is usually made in the Micronesian style, woven or tied into a flat collar.

The lei hibiscus flowers are tied Micronesian style into a lei like a collar.

White and lavender crown flowers are members of the milkweed family. There is a fine fiber in the stems which is used for fishing line. Leaves, bark and root are used as medicine for fever; larger amounts of the plant are poisonous. The sap can seriously burn eyes and skin.

Petals are removed and the little crown centers are strung singly (kui pololei), and the round lei is strung (kui poepoe).

Crown flower

pua kalaunu

In India crown flower is sacred. Kama, the Indian god of love, shoots his arrows into the hearts of mortals like Cupid. One of his darts is tipped with a crown flower. Ceremonial strands of crown flowers are hung in Indian temples and in Thailand are used for spirit offerings and in weddings. It is a popular belief that Liliuʻokalani, the last queen of Hawaiʻi, loved the crown flower best. She often wore many long strands of the miniature crowns, befitting a queen.

Queen Liliuʻokalani's statue is draped with crown flower lei, believed to be her favorite.

Chinese settlers brought pīkake to Hawaiʻi. It was a favorite plant for ornament, for scent, for flavoring jasmine tea. It is the national flower of the Philippines and Indonesia.

Pīkake
peacock, Arabian jasmine

In pageants and parades the queens and princesses may wear twenty strands of *pīkake* buds sixty or seventy inches long. *Pīkake* is dedicated to women and often worn by brides. The *pīkake lei* has taken on a romantic meaning in the Islands. One *lei*, or two, is friendly; three or four—a romance; five or six—I love you; more—you are a bride.

The single strands of pīkake are strung (kui pololei) and the thicker lei is strung round (kui poepoe).

A May Day Princess wears multiple strands and a crown of pīkake.

'Āinahau Palace at Waikīkī was the home of Ka'iulani's uncle, King Kalākaua.

Photo courtesy of Bishop Museum Archives.

Pīkake and the Princess

Dozens of peacocks roamed among the jasmine bushes on the 'Āinahau Palace grounds at Waikīkī. Ka'iulani, the last princess of the Hawaiian monarchy, grew up in the palace of her uncle, King Kalākaua. The young princess was attending boarding school in England when the king died and her Aunt Liliu'okalani assumed the throne in 1891.

News reached Princess Ka'iulani that the people of Hawai'i had revolted against the move to annex their kingdom to the United States. The queen was accused of treason and imprisoned in her palace. Ka'iulani left England for Washington to plead with President Grover Cleveland for her nation and her royal family. The President was swayed by the passionate 17-year-old girl, who was next in the line of succession to the throne. He urged Congress to restore the Monarchy and abandon the plan to annex Hawai'i. However, when he left office in 1897, Congress passed the resolution making Hawai'i a U.S. territory.

Princess Ka'iulani returned to her childhood home. Surrounded by the garden of sweet-smelling jasmine and the peacocks she loved, the last princess died. It was reported that the cause was a mysterious fever, but many believed it was a broken heart. The night she died her beloved peacocks screamed in grief in the palace garden. Since then both flower and bird are called *pīkake*.

Photo courtesy of the R.J. Baker Collection, Bishop Museum Archives.

Pua male
wedding flower, stephanotis, Madagascar jasmine, creeping tuberose

Daughters of the Polynesians favored white flowers for the *lei*. They brought a white ginger with them when they journeyed across the Pacific. Like her ancestors a Hawaiian bride will be adorned with sweetly perfumed white flowers on her wedding day. Her groom wears the open ended *maile lei*, the bride is draped with strings of ginger buds and jasmine. Several strands of *pīkake*, and *pua male*, the wedding flower, may crown her head and encircle her face.

Stephanotis, crown flower and pakalana *all belong to the milkweed family. Stephanotis vine comes from Madagascar.*

The Stephanotis is strung across the corolla in the circular pattern (kui poepoe). See p. 100.

Lei *sellers greet passengers on "Boat Day" at the Honolulu Harbor docks.*

Greeters performed hula *and sold their lei on the dock.*

Honolulu Lei Sellers

The arrival of a ship was cause for celebration and social events; family and friends meeting guests, press and photographers, music and *hula*. *Lei* sellers, arms draped with strands of *pakalana* and ginger, 'ilima and carnation, sold their *lei* for a quarter each on the pier.

Dora Brown Martinez sold *lei* with her mother on the Honolulu Harbor docks. "In boat days we could just go pick our flowers and leaves from the mountain, flowers were different from now. My favorite *lei* was the roses twined with *pīkake*. We had orchids and plumeria flowers, everything. In the old days a box cost $3, too expensive now."

As soon as airplanes began bringing visitors to Honolulu, *lei* sellers lined up along the road to the airport. On the back of old trucks, in junk cars, with tables and stands they displayed their *lei* for travelers arriving and departing the island. "Those *lei* sellers like my mom were the first Hawaiian entrepreneuers," says Dora's daughter, Fern Delos Santos.

The Territory of Hawai'i built 15 small thatched huts near the airport entrance on Lagoon Drive. *Lei* makers were invited to set up in 1952, and the same order in the line was kept. Those stands were named for the *lei* sellers, the location and order in line maintained over generations.

Today the names label the stalls next to the parking lot at Honolulu's inter-island terminal: Gladys, Rachael, Martha, Melia, Maile, Sophie, Harriet, Irene, Bessie, and Dora. "People ask me 'why you sitting here stringing those *lei*?' I tell them every flower I put on that needle makes people happy. When that *lei* makes you happy, it makes me happy." Dora is nearly 80 and mother of 14 children. "I was Grand Marshall for Aloha Week last year," she will proudly tell you. Dora was chosen to represent the theme "The *Lei*."

Before WW II lei *stands lined the road to the airport.*

Fern Delos Santos (left) and her mother, Dora Brown Martinez (right) stringing lei *at their Honolulu airport lei stand.*

Maunaloa
sea bean, *kauhi,* 'āwikiwiki, wild pea vine

The primitive custom of adorning with flowers has evolved to a high art with the *lei* makers of Hawai'i. When the settlers came from Europe and the Americas, Asia and the Pacific, some of them brought a new flowering tree or bush or vine. The *maunaloa lei* is testament to the ingenuity of the Hawaiian *lei* maker. If it smelled wonderful, or had no scent, didn't scratch or stink or stain, and held up for a time after picking, Hawaiians made it into a *lei*. Honolulu Harbor *lei* sellers grew the wild pea vines in their gardens to sew the deep pink blossoms into a beautiful design.

Maunaloa was introduced to the Islands in the last quarter of the nineteenth century. It cannot be exported.

Maunaloa buds are strung flat, alternating sides (kui lau). *See p. 101.*

The plumeria has a rubbery sap which is poisonous. Lubricating the lei needle with Vaseline makes stringing easier.

Plumeria

frangipani, *pua melia*, pagoda tree, temple flower

The "temple tree" is sacred in India and Sri Lanka, but was considered the "graveyard tree" in Hawai'i. Plumerias need little attention, provide shade for mourners, and shower the graves with sweet-smelling blossoms. When a Hawaiian died, the funeral took place within a day. If you needed a *lei* in a hurry the flowers were plentiful, easy to pick and quick to string.

Plumeria lei *single strung* (kui pololei).

Frangipani is found in warm countries from Indonesia to Polynesia to the Caribbean. Beautiful colors have been introduced and hybridized in Hawai'i. Plumeria flowers can smell like apricots or roses, like basil or lemon, wood and spice.

As soon as commercial aviation came to the Islands tourism swelled, and the demand for *lei* expanded. *Lei* sellers scrambled for any material they could string, and the plumeria was available and a long-lasting *lei* flower. Visitors loved the fragrance and the array of yellow, pink, red and "rainbow" plumerias. Older Hawaiians still call it *make*-man, dead man's *lei*.

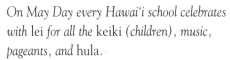

On May Day every Hawai'i school celebrates with lei for all the keiki (children), *music,* pageants, *and* hula.

Clusters of miniature green and yellow flowers from the milkweed family hang from the vines on trellises and fences in the summertime.

Pakalana
Chinese violet

Chinese settlers came to the Islands with many flowers the Hawaiians adopted for *lei* making. *Pakalana* is not a violet, but like violets it has a luscious, gentle scent which made it a favorite *lei* flower. Any *lei* with an alluring fragrance is a *lei* for love. Picking and stringing *pakalana* is a labor of love. A *lei* of many *pakalana* strands is preferred, and each one requires 150 blossoms.

Master *lei* maker Irmalee Pomroy recalls making her first *pakalana lei*. "I began by gathering the half-inch flowers that were growing on a chain-link fence that ran the length of the entrance road into the first elementary school where I taught. In preparation, I pulled the calyx from each *pakalana* blossom, only to discover that many had a honey bee stuck inside the tubular end of the flower. Some were still alive and happily flew away. Most were dead and had to be picked out of the flower. I was so saddened by this that it was several years later when I finally made another *pakalana lei*."

Hawaiians prefer to wear several strands of
pakalana, *each one made of 150 flowers.*

The pakalana lei *is single straight stringing*
(kui pololei) *by Cads Samio of Waimea.*

Lehua Pepa
paper flower, *lehua mau loa,* Globe amaranth, *bozu*

Six plants in the amaranth family grow in the Hawaiian Islands. Some amaranth are edible, some considered weeds. An "everlasting *lei*" is strung with the little flowers of one variety that look remarkably like clover. The purple, rose, and white "paper flowers" make a pretty *lei* fresh or dried.

Bozu meaning "bald head" is the name Japanese settlers gave the Globe amaranth (Gomphrena globosa).

Another amaranth which grows in Hawaiian forests is *pāpala*, a woody little shrub which once was used to make fireworks displays. Hawaiians would gather in their canoes to watch climbers atop the cliffs at Nāpali on Kaua'i throw lightweight sticks of flaming *pāpala* into the night sky. The sticks spun and swirled, tossed by the breeze, raining sparks mirrored in the water below.

Single strings (kui pololei) *of paper flower with a round lei* (kui poepoe) *arranged by color in a spiral pattern.*

Bougainvillea was brought to Hawai'i early in the nineteenth century and has flourished in the Islands. The little town of Hanapēpē on Kaua'i is surrounded by hillsides on fire with every shade of bougainvillea.

Bougainvillea

pukanawila, pua kepalō—devil's flower

On the Island of Hawai'i the intensity of its flaming colors caused islanders to name it devil's flower. The bracts are a riot of fiery colors like a Hawaiian sunset—orange, peach, pink, fuchsia, lavender, and purple. The white flowers are so tiny they are difficult to see, so it is the colorful bracts that attract the bees and birds. The *paniolos* (cowboys) on Hawai'i recognized bougainvillea, which comes from their home in Mexico.

The bougainvillea is tied in bunches and mounted on a braid for a hat lei.

Modern Lei

From the first "Boat Days" at the end of the nineteenth century, to the airport *lei* stands and big commercial *lei* production for the hospitality industry, the business of making and selling *lei* has mushroomed with Hawai'i's tourism. Dendrobium and vanda orchids are mass produced on commercial farms and imported from Thailand and Singapore. Thousands are needed for tourists, conventions, and film and television productions. Celebrations of Hawaiian history and culture during Aloha Week, and on May Day, which is *Lei* Day in Hawai'i, create a huge demand.

Cigar Flower

pua kīkā

The *Cuphea ignea* shrub from Mexico has been seen in Hawai'i since the late 1800's. Its scientific name means curved, fiery red—a perfect description of a cigar flower. Each tiny tube is ringed with grey, then white at the tip, like a miniature burning cigar. Bright red is not the only color; there are white cigar flowers and varieties the color of oranges and strawberries.

The *kīkā lei* is long-lasting and a marvel of the *lei* maker's work. In the first *Lei* Contest, May Day, 1928, Mrs. Peter Lee won the "Most Beautiful *Lei*" award for her complicated cigar flower *lei*. The patient stringers of these *lei* alternate the various colors of these petal-less flowers—red, white, orange. They string thousands of them in intricate patterns that resemble fine Indian beadwork.

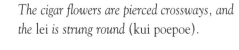

The cigar flowers are pierced crossways, and the lei *is strung round* (kui poepoe).

A tiny tube ringed with grey and white at its tip was named "cigar flower" by Hawaiians.

The firecracker flower is less than one inch long.

Firecracker

pahūpahū, firecracker vine, flame vine

This lowly cousin to the magnificent trumpet vine is considered quite common by Hawaiians. The small red flower with a yellow tip blooms year-round in gardens all over the Islands. Its scientific name is descriptive—Pyrostegia means "charming fire."

The firecracker *lei* is a fine example of the Hawaiian *lei* maker's artistic use of any material to make a *lei*, even what locals call "junk by the road." Maunakea Street *lei* shops display firecracker *lei* strung singly or crosswise in a variety of patterns—circular, spiral, side to side, or a chevron design. While the flower is not so highly regarded, it takes a skilled *lei* maker and hundreds of these tiny flowers to create the colorful designs.

The firecracker lei *is strung back-and-forth* (kui lau) *using 500 flowers.*

85

Maunakea Street

Lei stringing is pleasant labor taught to children and grandchildren, done by any Hawaiian who has a little free time. For many it has been a supplement to the family income, and for some, a family business for three or four generations.

Before World War II, Honolulu *lei* sellers parked by the curb near the Moana, Halekulani , and Royal Hawaiian Hotels in Waikīkī. They sold sweet-smelling garlands of plumeria and *'ilima* and *pīkake* out the window of a car, or from the back of their truck. In the 'fifties, selling *lei* on the downtown streets was outlawed, so sellers moved out to the airport road or set up their table on Maunakea Street in the Chinese district.

Vendors sold their lei from a parked car or truck until the 1950's when selling lei on the streets of Honolulu was outlawed.

Photo courtesy of Hawai'i State Archives.

Hawaiian *lei* makers used to sit along the sidewalks of Maunakea Street stringing and selling their *lei* from a basket. They hung their wares on the buildings, branches of a tree, or on a board with a row of nails. Today Maunakea Street is lined with *lei* shops, each one's merchandise a wildly-colored display of every kind of *lei*. Many of the *lei* makers' tables are visible from the sidewalk, where tourists are delighted to watch the fragrant flowers being strung in intricate patterns. Some of the shops have been taking orders for birthdays and graduations, weddings and openings, funerals and holidays for more than 50 years.

Lei makers sat along the sidewalk on Maunakea Street stringing their lei from baskets filled with flowers.

The dendrobium is mass produced in Hawai'i for commercial lei production.

Lei makers often name their designs, lei sellers give names to the lei as well. Dendrobium are strung in an amazing variety of patterns with names like "fish bone," "dragonfly," "crystal," "water lily," and "Christina."

Dendrobium Orchid
'okika, cane orchid, Thailand dendrobium, Red Soniya

This orchid is at home from India eastward into Asia and many Pacific islands. The long-lasting dendrobium has become the largest share of the commercial market in *lei* flowers. Available year 'round, in purples, pink, yellow, yellow-brown, green and white. Some have a faint scent, some no fragrance at all. The dendrobium is mass produced in Hawai'i, and imported from Thailand for commercial *lei* production.

A double dendrobium lei frames this beautiful Hawaiian face.

The amazing array of different methods of stringing dendrobium is the best example of the ingenuity of today's Hawaiian *lei* makers. Beth Garguilo is credited with the "Christina" *lei*, and several other dendrobium *lei* designs, all named for her children. New designs appear in competitions and *lei* shops, are copied and refined every year. Petals are removed or folded for some effects, or strung side to side. Sepals can be strung by themselves; so can the petals. The flowers are pierced through the lip, the nose, or the throat, in endless variations.

Vanda Orchid

'okika vanda, Vanda 'Miss Joaquim'

The Maoris of New Zealand say that the orchid did not come from the earth, but was created by the gods. Of the more than 20,000 species of orchids, only three are native to Hawai'i, and they are too rare to supply *lei* makers.

A vanda orchid *lei* was seen in the Honolulu May Day competition the first time in 1938. Nearly 10 years later it reappeared and won first prize. The *lei* maker, Mrs. Lee, made a beautiful design with the lavender-pink orchid shaped like a pansy. She created a flat *lei* which almost looks like it is braided, with soft ruffled edges. The *lei* was mis-named *"maunaloa"* because it looks similar to the wild pea flower *lei* of the same color. Both are strung *kui lau*, alternating sides, and are flat in the center. Since the 'forties this *"maunaloa*-style" has always been a very popular *lei*.

"Maunaloa-style" vanda lei is strung alternating side to side (kui lau) with its lateral petals removed.

Vanda once accounted for nearly one half of the wholesale *lei* and cut flowers market. In Hawai'i, 75 orchids are cultivated for their beauty and one other product—vanilla. Extracted from the seed pod of one variety, vanilla is an expensive crop imported mostly from Tahiti. Recently farms cultivating vanilla orchids have been started in Hawai'i. The growers are hoping for a new specialty food crop as successful as macadamia nuts and Hawaiian coffee.

The hybrid vanda orchid was introduced in 1930. The upright vines came to Hawai'i from the Singapore Botanical Gardens.

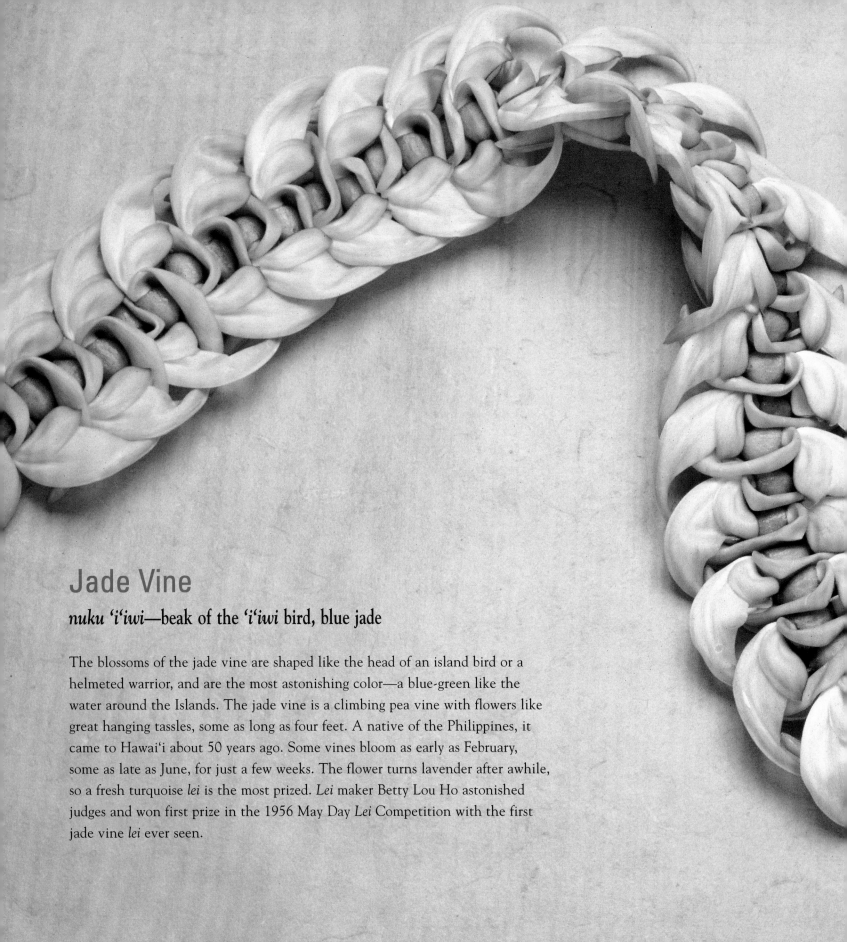

Jade Vine

nuku ʻiʻiwi—beak of the ʻiʻiwi bird, blue jade

The blossoms of the jade vine are shaped like the head of an island bird or a helmeted warrior, and are the most astonishing color—a blue-green like the water around the Islands. The jade vine is a climbing pea vine with flowers like great hanging tassles, some as long as four feet. A native of the Philippines, it came to Hawaiʻi about 50 years ago. Some vines bloom as early as February, some as late as June, for just a few weeks. The flower turns lavender after awhile, so a fresh turquoise *lei* is the most prized. *Lei* maker Betty Lou Ho astonished judges and won first prize in the 1956 May Day *Lei* Competition with the first jade vine *lei* ever seen.

The jade vine flower cannot be exported because of an insect that lives in its seed.

Hawaiians are excited about a newer arrival of the species which is a vibrant red-orange.

The jade lei is strung maunaloa-style, or crosswise, alternating side to side (kui lau) by David Chang of Kaua'i.

David's Jade

David Chang's family has lived for more than 100 years in Kōloa, the sugar mill town on the south side of Kaua'i. "My family were rice planters and merchants from China. My grandfather was born here, father born here. Our family had the store in town. We always worked for ourselves, not the plantation."

David spent time in Germany while he was in the army in the 1970's. It was a long way from Hawai'i. " I used to say to myself , 'every plant I remember that was unique, I will try to do on my land when I go back'. I would just think about that garden. The blue-green jade vine was most unique, I only knew one rich guy that had one. It looked like one of the best plants to make a fine *lei*. I got the plant from the Botanical Garden, every few years they will sell a few. Then you wait three years before it makes flowers."

"In Hawai'i if you go telling everyone you are going fishing, the fish will hear you and they won't bite. If you promise a jade *lei* to somebody the flowers won't grow, or I go and count flowers and I only get 70 when I need 90. Everyone knows David has the jade. I have the vine. I have the time." David says he has given thousands of jade *lei* over the years, "I don't do it for money, just give me some mangos or something."

"The blue jade is a very special *lei*. If somebody gives you a *lei* like this, you know they love you. They have to work hard, or pay a lot for the most expensive flower *lei*. Make somebody happy. They all say it's unbelievable, and they never forget that *lei*."

David explains while he "sews" the *lei*. "Pick the flowers early in the morning so they are hard. I lay out the flowers, check for bruises and choose the best side. Line up 90 flowers—half facing each way." David uses a heavy *lei* needle, pierces petal and calyx, alternating sides. He slides the flowers down the string four at a time, then ties a knot to keep the *lei* from twisting. "I tuck the point of the flower under along the edge to make the *lei* flat and smooth. That is my special touch. You have to close the *lei* on the person or it won't lay right."

To keep the *lei*, wrap in a damp paper towel, place in a zip lock bag in the refrigerator. Water will spot the blossoms, air will turn the *lei* purple.

How To Make *Lei*

Hawaiians have found many ways to attach flowers and greenery together to make their *lei*. Master *lei* maker Irmalee Pomroy says "there is no wrong way to make a *lei*." Everyone has a little trick or their own version of a design. Each method, practiced for generations, suits the flower, fern or vine, and the *lei* maker's talent and needs:

Wili

twisting the material itself; or twisting two or more strands together; or securing the material onto a foundation by winding or wrapping it with a wrapping strand.

Kīpu'u

pieces of the material are tied together.

Kui

stringing. Before they had needles Hawaiians used stiff grasses or the midrib of a coconut leaf to pierce the flowers and greens, and *hau* bast as thread. *Kui pololei* is stringing through the center of the flower lengthwise. *Kui poe poe*—round stringing with flowers pieced crosswise through the calyx or the corolla tube, and the flowers arranged in a circle facing out. *Kui lau* is stringing the flowers flat, through the calyx or stem and alternating the petals left and right.

Hili

braiding the material itself.

Micronesian-style

a two, three or four-strand plaiting technique borrowed from Western Pacific islands. Stems and blossoms are arranged flat, incorporated into the plait and secured with raffia or bast.

Haku (arrange in a braid)

Today any hat *lei* or *lei* for the head may be incorrectly called a *haku lei*. The word *haku* means to arrange or compose. A *haku mele* is a songwriter, *haku mo'olelo* a storyteller. Many misnamed *haku lei* are actually *wili* because the flowers and leaves are wrapped to secure them to a central cord. Some *lei*-making instructions include "mounting, mounting on a braid, and setting on a background" in their definition of *haku*. Some loosely consider it any *lei* where the flowers are attached to backing material.

For this book the *lei*-making term *haku* means to arrange in a braid. Flowers and leaves are secured by braiding ti leaf, dried banana stalk skin, *hau* bast, or raffia around the stems, incorporating the stems into the braid. *Lei* makers use an amazing variety of materials to make *haku*, usually with soft greens for backing and one, two, or several varieties of flowers in the design.

ti leaf *lei*: **wili**—twisting, winding

Wili is the term for twisting, winding, or wrapping. This *lei* is made by twisting the leaves into a strand, then winding two strands around each other. It is made with ti leaves which have been treated to make them pliable for twisting. Place the leaves on a towel shiny side up and iron them on medium-low setting—150 degrees—to make them supple. *Lei* makers use several methods to soften the leaves—some hold them over a direct flame, soak them in hot water, microwave them for one minute or even freeze them.

1. Wipe six to eight ti leaves clean and cut out the midrib. Reserving one-half leaf, cut the rest of your leaves into quarters at a 45-degree angle.

2. Tie the long segment and one of the shorter ones together one inch from the end. Secure the tied end by weighting it down with a brick, or use another pair of hands, or loop it around your big toe.

3. Twist each segment tightly in the same direction.

4. Wind the left segment around the right one like a rope. Add new leaf segments into the two twisted segments, leaving one inch of the end showing, and secure by twisting around it.

5. Continue twisting the leaf segments and adding to them until you have a 46" twisted strand. Tie the two ends together to close the *lei*.

loke lei: *wili*—wrapping

Wili is the term for twisting, winding, or wrapping. This *lei* is made by wrapping strips of raffia around short-stemmed materials and a backing or braid.

Alison Ah Puck always creates her pattern in threes. She makes clusters of three, six, or nine leaves of fern. She uses pink baby roses and green *loke lani* in threes, setting them in triangles on her *lei*.

1. Soak raffia in water. Cut three strips of raffia of even width to the measurement of the head or hat, plus 12". Knot them at one end and make a braid.

2. Cut leaves or fern tips 3" long and remove the bottom fronds to expose 1" stems. Tie a wrapping strand of raffia to the braid 6" from the top. Place six to nine fern tips on the braid and wrap it once.

3. Place one flower with 1" stem on the ferns, then wrap once. Tie a second flower and a fern tip below and to one side of the first flower. Wrap once, then add a third flower and fern tip to the opposite side wrap.

4. Add your second variety of flower in the same way, filling the spaces between them with fern tips. Continue your pattern until the *lei* is the desired length. Braid the ends of the raffia and trim to finish. Tie the *lei* closed, disguising the braided ends.

maile lei: *kīpuʻu*—tying, knotting

Kauaʻi *lei* makers use no less than three strands to make the maile *lei*, which is worn open-ended.

When *maile* is picked, the bark of the vine is grasped firmly and twisted to separate it from the core. With a sliding motion the bark and leaves are pulled from the core of the vine into a little cluster of leaves and crushed bark.

1. Choose two to four of the nicest tips of the *maile* for each strand. Smash the bark with a rock or hammer if the vine is too stiff to tie into a knot.

2. Stretch out the pieces of *maile*. Tie one or two maile tips to a length of *maile* to begin, then tie lengths of *maile* together to make a five-foot long strand.

3. Finish each strand with one or two of the nicest tips, then hold one end of all the strands together in one hand and twirl them like a lasso to combine the strands for the *lei*.

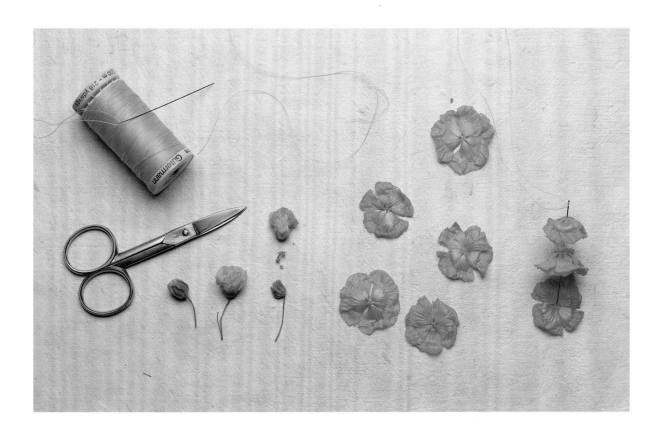

ʻilima lei: *kui pololei*—stringing

You will need 700 flowers, carpet thread, and a very thin needle. Some *lei* makers use a beading needle and quilting thread.

1. Pick the ʻilima flowers in the cool of the morning and allow them to open (about two hours). Gently pick off the green calyx and the tiny hard ovary. If the ovary does not come out easily, poke it with the needle.

2. Place the flowers face down on a soft surface—a sheet of craft store foam works well to keep the delicate blossoms from bruising.

3. Tie a knot 6" from the bottom of your thread. Pierce 10 flowers through the tiny hole, taking care not to tear the delicate petals. Pull the flowers down to the knot. Continue until you have a 36"-40" *lei*. Close the *lei* by tying the ends of the thread tightly; trim off excess thread.

stephanotis *lei*:   **kui poepoe**—stringing, double *lei*, circular pattern

You will need 175 flowers, a long *lei* needle, and heavy thread or string.

1. Cut the stephanotis corolla (tube) to 1/2" long.

2. Pierce the flower crosswise through the corolla. Add flowers, arranging three flowers in a circular pattern. Pull the flowers to the end of your string and keep adding in this way to the desired length, about 40".

maunaloa lei: **kui lau**—stringing back and forth or side to side

The *maunaloa* flowers must be picked before they open. You will need about 170 flowers, wet raffia or embroidery thread, a 10" *lei* needle or embroidery needle.

1. Pierce the calyx of the *maunaloa* with the petal pointing to the side. Add eight flowers, alternating sides, and gently pull them down the thread. Continue until you have a 36"-40" *lei*.

2. Allow the *lei* to "rest" until the petals soften—one or two hours. Fold each petal into the center of the *lei* covering the green calyx. Some *lei* makers use a thin strip of double-sided tape to keep the petals flat, but *lei* maker Lola Bukoski says that if you lay a table knife on the petals for awhile they will stay.

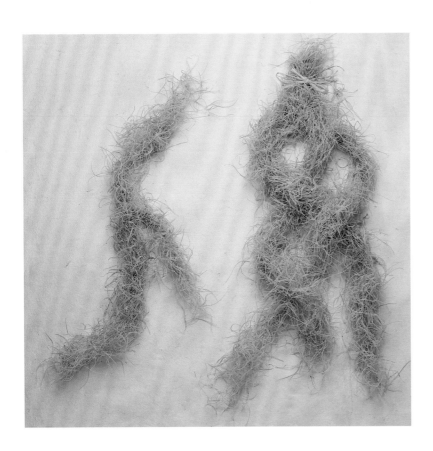

hinahina lei: **hili**—braiding, plaiting

1. Make three 40" lengths of the *hinahina* by twisting several strands together.

2. Tie the ends together with raffia and braid the three pieces. Tie the end together neatly with raffia.

Ginger bud *lei*: Micronesian style

You will need about 125 unopened ginger buds, tape and raffia.

1. Peel off the skin on the ginger bud—it has a sour smell.

2. Wet two strands of raffia two yards long. Tie a knot a few inches from the ends. Secure the raffia to a table with strong tape—carpet tape works well. Place a ginger bud between the two strands of raffia next to the knot as close to the petal as possible. Twist the bottom raffia over the top raffia.

3. Add the second bud, twist the raffia, then add a third bud, and twist the raffia again. Bend the stem of the first bud, placing it next to the fourth bud; twist the raffia around both.

4. Bend the second stem and place it next to the fifth bud, twist the strands of raffia. Continue adding buds and bending stems to create a 40-inch *lei* with a scalloped edge. To finish, bend two stems together, twist the raffia, bend the last stem and tie the raffia to secure it in place. Leave a few inches of raffia to close the *lei*.

Cover the *lei* with a sheet of plastic wrap and roll it to keep the buds pressed together. This will prevent the buds from opening before the *lei* is worn. Store in a closed container in the refrigerator.

$\mathcal{M}$arsha Heckman is a floral designer and lecturer who divides her time between Kaua'i and Mill Valley, California. Her previous books are *Bouquets: A Year of Flowers for the Bride* and *A Bride's Book.*

Photography by:

Ronnda Heinrich
Veronica Carmona

Additional Photography by:

Cat Sweeney
Jul-Lin Lum
Marsha Heckman
Ann Cecil
Jan Parker Soares